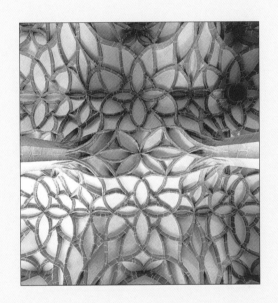

ERNST HAUSNER

AUSTRIA

INTRODUCTION
AND
REMINISCENCE

EDITION HAUSNER

The author is responsible for preparing
texts and pictures, and for the design,
layout and technical production supervision.

Translation into English by Gertrude Maurer.

Typeset and made up for printing on IBM Personal Computer.
IBM
Desktop-Publishing Oliver Hausner.

Colour separation and printing: Edelbacher Druck Ges.m.b.H., Vienna
Book binders: Gerald Frauenberger, Neudörfl
Typeface: 8/9/10 pt (Bauer) Bodoni
Paper: 150 g Magnostar of Leykam-Mürztaler
Papier- und Zellstoff-AG, Gratkorn.

ISBN 3-901141-05-7

This book has also been published in Chinese, French,
German, Italian, Japanese and Russian.

THE HISTORY

Venus of Willendorf, idol, made of limestone, c. 30,000 B.C., Naturhistorisches Museum, Vienna.

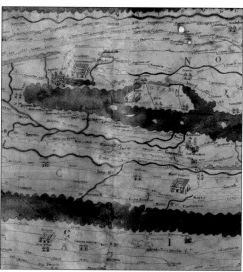

Roman road map, *Peutingeriana*, c. 370, top left: Vienna–Linz road section, Nationalbibiliothek.

The land in the heart of Europe that encompasses what is now known as the Republic of Austria was first settled in prehistoric times. Traces of continuous human habitation ever since have been established by archeological finds. The history of Austria and its role in the international context have been determined by its geographical location at the crossroads of ancient trading routes and interface of major European cultures – Germanic, Slavic and Roman. Evolving from a small nucleus state that guarded the eastern frontier of Western Europe at the beginning of the second millennium, Austria became a political power that grew steadily over the centuries, its sovereigns assuming the mantle of Holy Roman emperors, transforming their country into the Austro-Hungarian Empire, a multinational state and major player on the European stage until, early in the 20th century, it disintegrated, leaving behind a small republic on what remained of the vast territories of former times.

The oldest traces left by man on Austrian territory were found on mountainous terrain and date back to the Palaeolithic Age (150,000 to 80,000 B.C.). The valley of the Danube and its immediate vicinity were settled by 10,000 B.C. The culture of its inhabitants, still nameless as a people, speaks to us through treasures that the soil yields to archaeologists (*Venus of Willendorf* in the Wachau). A seismic shift of the climate toward the end of the Ice Age led to broad cultural changes, the transformation of the hunter and gatherer society to

farming and lifestock production, and the emergence of permanent settlements.

With ores and salt mined in the eastern Alps (3rd and 4th millennia B.C.), trade spreading across the Alpine passes to the south, and a stratified society evolving in the communities (artisans, peasants, warriors), a Central European culture came into being in the 2nd millennium B.C., the so-called "urnfield culture". It was followed by the Iron Age (c. 700 to 15 B.C.), named after the newly discovered working material which brought the breakthrough of a new culture. Its transitional phase is known as "Hallstatt period" from the necropolis at Hallstatt in Upper Austria, long a centre of salt mining. When Celtic tribes moved into the lands of the eastern Alps around 400 B.C., they brought with them a culture of their own (La Tène). The Noricans, a leading Celtic tribe, formed a kingdom (Regnum Noricum, centred in Carinthia) that was the first regular state on Austrian soil. Closely linked to its affluent neighbour in the south (Noric iron, open-pit mining at the Styrian Erzberg), thoroughly Romanised and dependent on the Romans, it was finally absorbed in the Empire (15 B.C.) in a strategic move by the Romans. The Roman provinces of Raetia, Noricum and Pannonia established on Noricum's territory served as buffers to protect the Imperium against the onslaught of Germanic tribes thrusting south from the north of Europe. Over the next 400 years, the precursors of places sprang up that are important today: Vindobona-

Strettweg Chariot, c. 600 B.C., found in the grave of a prince of the Hallstatt period, Joanneum, Graz.

Vienna, Iuvavum-Salzburg, Brigantium-Bregenz. The provinces were under the sway of Roman culture and religion, civilisation and administration (earliest traces of Christianity from the 2nd century). The civil city of Vindobona numbered 15,000 inhabitants; to its east, Carnuntum (now Petronell) at the Danube grew to be the largest Roman settlement on Austrian soil.

The Empire of the West ultimately succumbed to successive waves of Germanic, Eastern European and Asiatic peoples and tribes who, in pushing south, kept supplanting and subduing each other. By the middle of the 6th century, the great migratory movement had extinguished the last remnants of Roman civilisation on Austrian territory.

Over the next centuries, the Bavarians, a land-tilling tribe from Western Europe, advanced their territory to the east, constantly in collision with the nations from the East (Avars, Slavs and Magyars), settling and Christianising Austria in the process. Charlemagne, king of the Franks, subjugated their land; the "Carolingian colonisation" and a decisive victory over the Avars and Slavs laid the foundation for the Carolingian's Avarian Mark along the banks of the river Danube.

The border mark was lost to the Magyars but was restored after their defeat (955) at the hand of Otto I, king of the Germans, as an independent margravate known as Ottonian Mark. Located along the Danube, it abutted the Carantanian Mark in the south of Austria. In 976, the

German emperor invested the Babenbergs, a Bavarian family of colonisers, with the fief of the Ottonian Mark (extending from the eastern banks of the Enns to the vicinity of the Traisen). The area became the nucleus of Austria and was first referred to as "ostarrichi" in a title deed of 996.

Under Frederick I Barbarossa, the margravate was elevated to the rank of duchy and granted considerable independence by his imperial decree *Privilegium minus* (1156). It grew into a Central European power through territorial acquisitions in the east (Magyars, frontier along March and Leitha), bequests (Duchy of Styria, 1192) and the political skills of a dynasty that ruled for 270 years. Around 1150, Vienna became the residency of the dukes; by the end of the century, the territory was settled and converted to Christianity. The monasteries founded in the process made an eminent contribution to securing the dominion and went on to develop into centres of culture and civilisation that maintained their importance for centuries.

When the last of the Babenberg dukes was slain fighting against the Hungarians in 1246, the duchy was drawn into the power struggle between its neighbours, succumbing to King Ottocar II of Bohemia in 1252. His rule, widely accepted and successfully consolidating the country, extended from Bohemia to the Adriatic Sea.

Such an accumulation of power was soon to collide with the claims and aspirations of Rudolf von Habsburg, who had been chosen German king in 1273. The

Emperor Frederick III, detail of the slab of his Gothic sarcophagus, 1457–1513, Stephansdom.

consequent contest of wills ended with the Bohemian king's death in the Battle of Dürnkrut in 1278. The Babenberg domain accrued to King Rudolf I who founded a dynasty that would rule Austria for more than 600 years. In 1282, Rudolf von Habsburg invested his two sons Albert and Rudolf with the duchies of Austria (below the Enns) and Styria.

Forced to cede some of their possessions in Switzerland, the Habsburgs recouped their losses by acquiring Tyrol and parts of the Wendic Mark under Duke Rudolf IV, a political animal of the highest order. Milestones of his rule (1348–65) were the foundation of Vienna University, reconstruction of St. Stephen's Cathedral in Vienna in the Gothic style, and the forgery of a document known as *Privilegium maius* to prove that he and his family were of higher rank than the German emperor. His subjects were visited with an infestation of locusts, crop failures and the black death in 1348/49 which claimed one third of the entire population of Europe.

Notwithstanding political strive, civil war, bickering between the estates, Turkish invasions, the division of Austria into three Habsburg dynasties and their family squabbles, Frederic III was able to re-unite his possessions in the course of his reign of 53 years (Holy Roman Emperor in 1452). From his time the imperial dignity continued almost hereditary (with a single exception) in the House of Austria for more than 350 years. When under Frederic's son Maximilian I (1493–1519) the Middle Ages

gave way to the Renaissance, Habsburg's rule already extended across vast stretches of land. Diplomatic skills and well-considered marriages procured him Burgundy, parts of Upper Italy, Hungary and Bohemia, Spain and Portugal, together with their overseas colonies. The dynasty divided into two lines: Austrian-German and Dutch-Spanish; and Charles V (king of Spain from 1516) proudly reigned over an empire in which "the sun did not set".

From the early 16th century, the spirit of enlightenment wrought deep-going social changes and brought about the blossoming of the sciences and arts. Administrative reforms were introduced to revise the organisational structures of the Habsburg dominions; the invention of moveable type for printing encouraged the spread of knowledge and new ideas – including the tenets of Luther's reformation among his adherents in the empire of the Catholic Habsburgs. Religious disputes and their political consequences, the wretched situation of a destitute peasantry and, not least, a dearth of morals among Catholic clergy combined to incite especially cruel and brutish bloodshed and gave rise to rigorous campaigns by the forces of the Counter-Reformation. Religious hostilities soon turned into an outright battle for power on the European stage in the Thirty Years' War, which left terrible devastation and destruction in its wake.

Antagonism and discord between the Habsburg dominions (including friction between the estates and the sovereign)

First mention of Austria "ostarrichi", deed by Emperor Otto III, 996, Hauptstaatsarchiv, Munich.

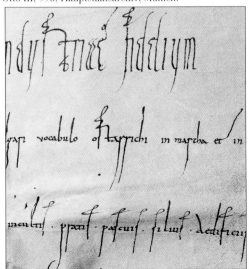

Decapitation of the leaders of the estates, in Wiener Neustadt, 1522, Stadtarchiv Wiener Neustadt.

Siege of Vienna 1683, *Engagement of the Relief Army*, contemporary painting, F. Geffels, Historisches Museum.

French bombardment of Vienna, 11 and 12 May 1809, engraving by P. Piringer, Historisches Museum.

Emperor Charles VI was the last of the male Habsburgs. His "Pragmatic Sanction", which provided for the inseparability of the hereditary lands and female succession, allowed his daughter Maria Theresa (1740–80) to ascend the throne. In two long wars she preserved her sovereign rights and her dominions with the exception of Silesia. Married to Francis Stephen of Lorraine (crowned German emperor in 1745) and devoted mother of 16 children, she shaped the history of Austria with her remarkable personality, her reforms of the administrative, military, tax and school systems governed by the principles of enlightened absolutism, and her mercantilistic encouragement of industry and commerce. Her reforms were continued by her son Joseph II, co-regent from 1765 and ruler in his own right in 1780–90. He abolished serfdom, granted religious toleration and suppressed monasteries which did not serve the common weal (schools, hospitals). At their lifetimes, Vienna emerged as a capital of European music (Ch. W. Gluck, J. Haydn and W. A. Mozart).

Around 1800, Austrian statecraft was dominated by the endeavour to sustain and defend the old order against the refractory ideas of the French Revolution. In ever changing coalitions, the powers of Europe struggled against the spread of the revolution and against Napoleon. When Napoleon crowned himself emperor of France in 1804, Francis I of Habsburg retaliated by assuming the title of emperor of Austria; the Holy Roman Empire ceased to exist in

Maria Theresa and Francis I Stephen, life-size oil painting by P. Kobler, 1746, St. Florian Abbey.

frustrated any effective defense against the Turks who, after conquering Constantinople, were becoming a consistent thorn in the flesh of Central Europe. In 1529 and again in 1683, Turkish armies appeared before Vienna, and the city's defenders were hard put to throw off the siege and check the Turkish progress. In several campaigns following 1683, Prince Eugene of Savoy, commander of three Habsburg emperors, secured ultimate victory over the "foe of Christendom" (which was supported and succoured by the French).

With Austria now securely installed as a principal European power, absolutism and the Catholic Church, having carried the day in the Counter-Reformation, reigned triumphant in Habsburg's domains. The claim of universal power pertaining to the court, church and nobility, all of whom had recently succeeded to great fortunes, found its expression in a new lifestyle, the Baroque. Its external manifestation sought to glorify the victories of Emperor and Church in a marriage of art and culture embodied in a host of splendid churches, monasteries, abbeys, palaces and stately homes. Vienna, capital of the empire and residency of its sovereign, was converted into the magnificent centre of a powerful realm. When the Spanish line became extinct at the end of the 17th century, Spain and its colonies were lost to France in the War of the Spanish Succession, but its secondary territories – the Low Countries, Sardinia, Milan, Naples and Mantua – were appropriated by Austria.

1806. Napoleon's campaigns inflicted several disastrous defeats upon Austria (cession of territories, heavy money indemnity); Vienna was captured in 1804 and again in 1809. It was not until Napoleon was finally vanquished in the Battle of Waterloo that the Congress of Vienna (Metternich) could set about restoring Europe to its former balance of power.

The shape of events in the first half of the 19th century was controlled by government measures (censorship, police state) designed to shore up and protect existing regimes against incendiary ideas as much as by the speed of ongoing technological progress. The spread of steam engines and other novel machinery engendered the explosive growth of industrial production; railways revolutionised the transport system. The growing number of factory workers was forged into a new estate: the working class. The bourgeoisie continued to be excluded from the business of government and withdrew into a private sphere of its own. Classicism and Romantic Revival metamorphosed into the *Biedermeier*, the celebration of private life expressed in painting (F. Waldmüller, M. v. Schwind, R. v. Alt), music (L. van Beethoven, F. Schubert, J. Strauss) and literature (F. Grillparzer, F. Raimund, J. Nestroy).

Total repression of all political aspirations and tensions between the national groups were relieved by the upheaval of 1848. Starting in March, bourgeois, workers and students took to the streets and achieved at least partial successes – abolition of censorship, liberation of the peasants (from soccage and tithe) – before the turbulences were subdued in October. With the conservative forces returned to power, 18-year-old Francis Joseph assumed the throne in 1848, originally ruling as an absolute sovereign and holding his office for almost 70 years. Constant domestic pickering between the nationalities, political calamities and military defeats compelled him to cede territories in Italy and to Prussia (1866) and precluded Austria from exerting any further influence on the development of Germany.

In 1867, the *Ausgleich* granted Hungary equal status, fusing the agglomerate state into the Austro-Hungarian Empire. In the liberal era that followed, gradual progress was made in anchoring fundamental rights in the constitution and improving the situation of the labouring masses who lived in destitution and squalor. Political parties emerged (Social Democrats and Christian Social Party) and in 1907 universal, equal, direct and secret suffrage was obtained (except for women).

A flourishing economy towards the end of the 19th century (*Gründerzeit*) vented its energy on the generous development of the imperial capital in the new Historicist style (Ring). Art, culture and science attained a new pinnacle at the turn of the century in spite (or because) of the countless rifts and tensions that tore at the very fabric of society (industrialisation, emergence of a proletariat), laying the foundations of modernity. The age was dominat-

Twilight of the monarchy at the turn of the century, *Court Ball*, W. Gause, 1900, Historisches Museum.

ed by the likes of O. Wagner and A. Loos (architecture), G. Klimt, E. Schiele, O. Kokoschka and A. Egger-Lienz (painting), J. Brahms, A. Bruckner, G. Mahler and A. Schönberg (music), A. Schnitzler, H. v. Hofmannsthal (literature) and S. Freud (psychiatry's founding father).

When Crown Prince Francis Ferdinand was assassinated in Sarajevo in 1914, the national collapse and disintegration, long looming on the horizon, precipitated the First World War, a ferocious engagement between the European powers that took four years to decide. It terminated in the annihilation of the multinational Austro-Hungarian Empire, its disembodiment into many national states, a complete revision of the Central European map and the founding of the Republic of Austria out of the remains of a great European power.

The new Republic withstood the tribulations of its tumultuous first years. But its beneficial development was soon arrested by clashes between the armed adherents of two camps, the Social Democratic *Schutzbund* and the bourgeois *Heimwehr*, who became increasingly radicalised by the ideological tensions following a lost war. In reaction to the Social Democrat rising of 1927, a conservative-authoritarian regime was installed in 1933, which suspended parliamentary government and asserted itself against the Social Democrats in a civil war in February 1934, but lost its chancellor to Nazi putschists in June.

In the wake of these traumatic events Austria was increasingly drawn into the

embrace of the German Reich, which at that time was still successfully run by the Nazis under Adolf Hitler, and finally lost its struggle to maintain political independence. Following an ultimatum, it was entered by German troops on 12 March 1938. The *Anschluss* was confirmed by a referendum in April. Austria ceased to exist as a single unity in 1939 (Ostmark). The Second World War that began in the same year claimed vast numbers of victims on all sides until fighting stopped in 1945. Towards the end, the battle lines had reached Austrian soil, and they left behind a country divided into Russian, American, British and French occupation zones.

After 1945, Austria set about reconstructing the country and its economy, a feat made possible by the firm belief of Austrians in the viability of their country and the co-operation between all democratic parties. In spite of the confrontation between the superpowers (East-West conflict, Cold War), Austria had its independence restored when the State Treaty was signed in Vienna on 15 May 1955.

Today, the people of Austria understand themselves as natural guardians of a great heritage within the narrow confines of the current borderlines. Ancient cultural ties, tolerance and openness, driven by the wellsprings of its history and its location in the heart of Europe, are just a few of the prerequisites that make for a promising future for Austria in the heart of a continent that experiences momentous political and social change at the end of the 2nd millennium.

The signatories of the Austrian State Treaty, 15 May 1955, balcony of the Belvedere in Vienna.

Revolution of 1848, 13 March, students getting arms from the armoury Am Hof, Heeresgeschichtliches Museum.

11 · BURGENLAND   19 · CARINTHIA   27 · LOWER AUSTRIA

37 · UPPER AUSTRIA   47 · SALZBURG   57 · STYRIA

67 · TYROL   77 · VORARLBERG   85 · VIENNA

BURGENLAND

1 · At the Seewinkel.

2 · Near Bernstein.

3 · Lockenhaus Castle.

4 · Near the western shore of Neusiedler See.

5 · Storm brooding over Neusiedler See near Rust.

6 · Schlaining Castle.

7 · Stadtschlaining, Catholic parish church, interior.

8 · Frauenkirchen, pilgrimage church.

9 · "Fishermen's Church", Rust.

10 · Eisenstadt, city hall.

11 · Forchtenstein Castle.

12 · Schloss Esterházy, ceremonial hall, Eisenstadt.

13 · Schloss Deutschkreutz, arcaded courtyard.

14 · Arcade, Unterwart.

15 · Flag throwing, Neckenmarkt.

16 · Potter, Stoob.

17 · Tamboura band, Stinatz.

18 · Stork family, Apetlon.

19 · Corpus Christi Day, Steinberg/Rabnitz.

20 · Schloss Kobersdorf, inner courtyard.

21 · Grape harvest, Rust.

22 · Eisenstadt, Joseph Haydn-Gasse.

23 · Back alley, Mörbisch.

24 · View from Halbturn across Seewinkel.

25 · Southern aspect, Günser Gebirge.

26 · Güssing Castle, sunrise.

27 · View across Neusiedler See towards Schneeberg.

CARINTHIA

1 · View from Dobratsch towards Klagenfurt basin.

2 · Grossglockner, Pasterze glacier.

3 · Mountain vista near Innerfragant.

4 · Near St. Veit an der Glan.

5 · Hochosterwitz Castle.

6 · Klagenfurt, Alter Platz.

7 · Alp near Mallnitz.

8 · Gmünd, town gate at the Malta.

9 · St. Veit an der Glan, town square.

10 · Millstätter See.

11 · Apriach, Möll valley and Eichhorn falls.

12 · Spittal an der Drau, Schloss Porcia, arcaded courtyard.

13 · Maria Wörth, Wörther See.

23

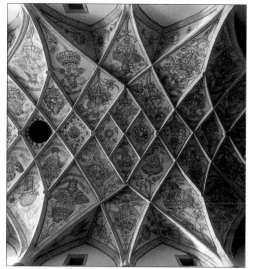

14 · Maria Saal, pilgrimage church, vault.

15 · Thörl-Maglern, parish ch., Goth. frescos.

16 · Ossiach, former abbey church, vault.

17 · Maria Gail, parish church, Gothic altar.

18 · The ducal throne on Zollfeld.

19 · Bad St. Leonhard, par.ch., Goth.window.

20 · Gurk, cathedral church, crypt.

21 · Heiligenblut, parish church, Gothic altar.

22 · Kötschach-Mauthen, parish ch., vault.

23 · Klagenfurt, estates' house, heraldic hall.

24 · Millstatt, former abbey church, Gothic Lenten veil.

25 · Western aspect of the Gerlitzen, Southern Limestone Alps.

26 · View from Dobratsch to the Karnic Alps.

27 · Viktring, former abbey church, high altar, Gothic glass windows.

1 · Near Mannersdorf, Vienna basin.

2 · Semmering, Raxalpe.

3 · Near Kirchschlag, Bucklige Welt.

4 · Poppy field near Rastenberg, Waldviertel.

5 · Prospect of Seitenstetten Abbey, Mostviertel.

6 · Retz, view from the tower.

7 · Krems, Stein parsonage.

8 · Schloss Petronell.

9 · St. Pölten, city square.

10 · Schloss Heiligenkreuz-Gutenbrunn, staircase.

11 · Korneuburg, weekly market on the town square.

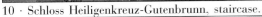

12 · Langenlois, Kornmarkt, plague column.

13 · Schloss Schallaburg.

31

14 · Farmhouse near Waidhofen an der Ybbs.

15 · Western aspect of Aggstein and the Danube.

16 · View across the Pulkau valley towards Staaz Castle.

17 · Wildendürnbach, line of winepressing houses.

18 · View from Josefsberg towards Ötscher.

19 · Pulka, Heiligblutkirche, Gothic altar.

20 · Klosterneuburg Abbey, ceremonial hall.

21 · Herzogenburg, abbey church, organ.

22 · Melk, abbey church, vault.

23 · Schöngrabern, par.ch., Roman. reliefs.

24 · Geras Abbey, library, dome fresco.

25 · Zwettl, abbey church, choir.

26 · Seitenstetten Abbey, marble hall.

27 · Heiligenkreuz, abbey church, choir.

28 · Altenburg, abbey church, vault.

29 · Melk Abbey, library.

30 · Eggenburg, parish church, Gothic vault.

31 · St. Valentin, parish church, Gothic vault.

32 · Göttweig Abbey, staircase.

UPPER AUSTRIA

1 · View from Ameis-Berg towards the Bohemian Forest.

2 · View across the valley basin of Windischgarsten towards Bosruck.

3 · Prospect of Vorderer Langbath-See, Höllengebirge.

4 · View from Schef-Berg across the Innviertel.

5 · View from Schafberg across Mondsee towards Irrsee.

39

6 · Freistadt, town square.

7 · Aschach, Danube quay.

8 · Obernberg am Inn, market square.

9 · Hallstatt, Hallstätter See.

10 · Steyr, old town and town square.

11 · Schärding, Oberer Stadtplatz, Silberzeile.

12 · Linz, view from the city square towards Pöstlingberg.

13 · Wels, town square.

41

14 · Farmhouse near Grieskirchen.

15 · Schloss Greinburg, arcaded courtyard.

16 · Schloss Schwertberg.

17 · Farmhouse near Kronstorf.

18 · View from Schafberg towards Dachstein.

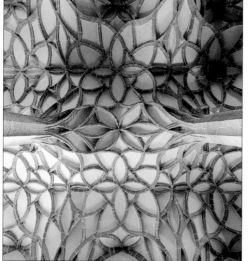
19 · Königswiesen, parish church, vault.

20 · Schlierbach, abbey church.

21 · Engelszell, abbey church, ceiling fresco.

22 · Stadl-Paura, parish church, dome.

23 · St. Wolfgang, parish church, altar.

24 · St. Florian Abbey, library.

25 · Reichersberg, abbey ch., ceiling fresco.

26 · Spital am Pyhrn, former abbey church.

27 · Steyr, parish church, vault.

28 · Wilhering, abbey church.

29 · Rustic cabinet from Gunskirchen.

30 · Scharnstein, scythe-smith's workshop.

31 · Ried im Innkreis, lifestock auction hall.

32 · Grein, historical town theatre.

SALZBURG

1 · Near Postalm.

2 · Near Lungötz, Tennengebirge.

3 · Prospect of the Glockner mountain road.

4 · Prospect of Maria Pfarr, Niedere Tauern.

5 · Alp on Hochkönig, Mandlwand.

6 · Hallein, town square.

7 · Salzburg, old court pharmacy.

8 · Dienten am Hochkönig, Haus Am Platz.

50

9 · Salzburg, cemetery of St. Peter.

10 · Salzburg, old town and Hohensalzburg Fortress.

11 · Salzburg, Getreidegasse.

12 · Salzburg, Mirabellgarten.

13 · Salzburg, Schloss Hellbrunn, music room.

14 · Hohenwerfen Fortress.

15 · Schloss Goldegg, knights' hall, murals.

16 · Farmhouse, Reith bei Lofer, Pinzgau.

17 · Near Hinterthal, Steinernes Meer.

18 · View from Schafberg across the Osterhorn peaks towards Untersberg.

19 · Mauterndorf Castle, Romanesque chapel.

20 · Salzburg, Franziskanerkirche, vault.

21 · Irrsdorf, Gothic church portal.

22 · Maria Plain, pilgrimage ch., high altar.

23 · Tamsweg, St. Leonhard, Rom. knocker.

24 · Oberalm, parish church, high altar.

25 · Michaelbeuern Abbey, winter choir.

26 · Salzburg, Cathedral, domical vault.

27 · Salzburg, Franziskanerkirche, high altar.

28 · Hohensalzburg Fortress, prince-bishop's suite, Goldene Stube, Gothic state room.

29 · Krimml waterfalls.

30 · Salzburg, Schloss Hellbrunn, pleasance.

31 · Historical grain shed, Lasaberg, Lungau.

32 · Loferer Steinberge at the Strub pass.

STYRIA

1 · At the South Styrian Wine Road.

2 · View across the Salza valley towards Hochschwab.

3 · View across the Enns valley towards Dachstein.

4 · Near Riegersburg, Eastern Styria.

5 · Near Admont, at the mouth of the Gesäuse, a narrow passage of the Enns valley.

6 · Leoben, Baroque burgher's house.

7 · Bruck an der Mur, fountain, Gothic burgher's house.

8 · Murau, upper Mur valley.

9 · Straden, Eastern Styria.

10 · Graz, city hall.

11 · Graz, estates' house, arcaded courtyard.

12 · Vordernberg, historical ironworks.

13 · Frohnleiten an der Mur.

61

14 · Strechau Castle, arcaded courtyard.

15 · Farmhouse in Western Styria, Tomberg.

16 · Farmhouse in Upper Styria, Buchauer Sattel.

17 · Graz, Schloss Eggenberg, ceremonial hall.

18 · Riegersburg.

19 · Göss, former abbey church, vault.

20 · Hartberg, Romanesque charnel-house.

21 · Gaishorn, parish church, vault.

22 · Vorau Abbey, library.

23 · Krakauhintermühlen, St. Ulrich chapel.

24 · Rein Abbey, abbey church.

25 · Fernitz, pilgrimage church, vault.

26 · Mariazell, pilgrimage church, organ.

27 · St. Georgen ob Murau, parish ch., vault.

64

28 · Admont Abbey, library.

29 · Wies, Western Styria, pumpkin pitting.

30 · Seebach, old farmer's mill.

31 · Frauenberg bei Admont, pilgrimage church.

32 · Eisenerz, Baroque burgher's house.

TYROL

1 · In the Virgental, East Tyrol.

2 · Kühtai, high valley.

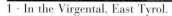

3 · View from Kirchdorf in Tirol towards Wilder Kaiser.

4 · Paznaun valley near Galtür.

5 · View across the upper Inn valley near Landeck.

6 · Vicinity of Zwieselstein, Ötz valley, near Timmelsjoch.

7 · Innsbruck, Helblinghaus, façade detail.

8 · Walchsee, inn, façade detail.

9 · Schwaz, old town, Franz-Josef-Strasse.

10 · Holzgau, façade.

11 · Farmhouses in the Paznaun valley.

12 · Innsbruck, old town, Herzog Friedrich-Strasse.

13 · Holzgau, façade detail.

14 · Stans, Schloss Tratzberg, Gothic murals.

15 · Innsbruck, old estates' house, session hall.

16 · Innsbruck, Hofburg, giants' hall.

17 · Innsbruck, Schloss Ambras, painted wood ceiling.

18 · Innsbruck, Schloss Ambras, Spanish hall.

19 · St. Georg ob Tösens, Gothic murals.

20 · Schwaz, parish church, vault.

21 · Rattenberg, parish church, vault.

22 · Wilten, parish church, interior.

23 · Procession of the Sacred Heart, Grins.

24 · Götzens, parish church, interior.

25 · Stams, abbey church, interior.

26 · Volders, Karlskirche, dome.

27 · Innsbruck, Hofk., tomb of Maximilian I.

74

28 · Innsbruck, Domkirche, interior.

29 · Wenns, Platzhaus, façade detail.

30 · Nauders, upper Inn valley, crocus meadow.

31 · On the Hahntennjoch.

32 · Farmhouse, Ausservillgraten.

VORARLBERG

1 · In the Bregenz Forest near Damüls.

2 · View from Fontanella towards the Arlberg mountains.

3 · Siberian iris, Bangser Ried near Feldkirch.

4 · Lech am Arlberg.

5 · Schröcken am Hochtannberg, Braunarlspitze.

6 · Mountain farm near Warth.

7 · Bregenz, upper town, Deuringschlösschen.

8 · Near Au im Bregenzerwald, Kanisfluh.

9 · Feldkirch, view from Schattenburg Castle.

10 · Dornbirn, market square, Rotes Haus.

11 · Farmhouse in Gaschurn, Montafon.

12 · Hohenems, palace, inner courtyard.

13 · View from Fraxern across the Rhine valley.

14 · Damüls, parish church, Gothic mural.

15 · Damüls, parish church, interior.

16 · Bregenz, St. Gallus, ceiling fresco.

17 · Braz, parish church, altars.

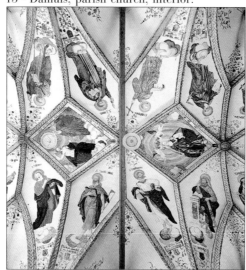

18 · Ludesch, St. Martin, vault.

19 · Feldkirch, Schattenburg, inner courtyard.

20 · Ludesch, St. Martin, Gothic murals.

21 · Bregenz, St. Gallus, interior.

22 · Feldkirch, Schattenburg, Goth. chamber.

23 · Farmhouse near Raggal, Grosses Walsertal valley.

24 · Farmhouse, Au im Bregenzerwald.

25 · Burgher's house, Dornbirn, market square.

26 · Inn, Bezau im Bregenzerwald.

27 · Bregenz, upper town, old town hall.

1 · Rooftops at Griechengasse-Fleischmarkt.

2 · Michaelerplatz, Michaelertor, Hofburg.

3 · View across Rathauspark and Volksgarten towards Hofburg.

4 · View from Platz Am Hof towards Stephansdom.

5 · View from Stock-im-Eisen-Platz across Graben towards Kohlmarkt.

6 · Palais Pallavicini, ceremonial hall.

7 · Palais Trautson.

8 · Unteres Belvedere towards Oberes Belvedere.

9 · Hofburg, Amalienburg, Alexander-Appartement.

10 · Palais Kinsky, staircase.

11 · Schloss Schönbrunn, grand gallery (ceremonial hall).

12 · Prince Eugen's winter palais, staterooms.

13 · Schloss Schönbrunn, gardens, grand parterre.

14 · Grosser Musikvereinssaal, New Year's Concert.

15 · State Opera House, staircase.

16 · Burgtheater, southern staircase.

17 · Hofburg, Spanish Riding School.

18 · Nationalbibliothek, grand hall, dome.

19 · Universitätskirche.

20 · Piaristenkirche, dome.

21 · Kirche Am Hof, Virgin Mary's column.

22 · Karlskirche, dome.

23 · Universitätskirche, *trompe-d'œil* dome.

24 · Dominikanerkirche, vault.

25 · Jugendstil residential building, Wienzeile.

26 · Altlerchenfelder Kirche, vault.

27 · Church Am Steinhof.

92

28 · Stephansdom, vault.

29 · View from the Danube Canal towards Stephansdom.

30 · Auditorium of the State Opera House, Opera Ball.

31 · View across Wurstelprater towards Stephansdom.

32 · Dead Danube channel, Prater forest.

The Republic of Austria is a Central European, landlocked country,
its longitude lying between 9°32' (westernmost point)
and 17°10' (easternmost point) east of Greenwich,
and its latitude between 49°1' (northernmost point)
and 46°22' (southernmost point) north.
The national territory extends 573 km from east to west,
and 294 km from north to south.
The frontier of 2,706 km in length encloses 83,858 sq km of Austrian soil
which ranges in altitude from 3,797 m in the Central Alps (Grossglockner)
to 115 m above sea level at the edges
of the Great Hungarian Plain (Neusiedler See).
The Austrian landscape has distinct regional characteristics:
in the north the Bohemian massif, a plateau of granite and gneiss rock;
the Alpine and Carpathian foothills to its south and southeast;
the Alps (60% of the total area), the Vienna basin and
the fringes of the Great Hungarian Plain to the east.
Of the territory, forest makes up some 41%; arable land, grassland,
gardens and vineyards together have 36%, and alpine pastures take 11%.
Two-fifths of the territory are used as permanent settlement areas.
With several Central European geographical regions overlapping in Austria,
the country's climate and vegetation reflect the
(rather wet) Atlantic influence in the west and the
(rather dry) continental-Pannonian weather in the east;
with a separate climatic zone in the inner Alps
(short summers, long winters, plenty of precipitation).
The wealth of landscapes provides habitats for an abundant flora
and fauna that is particularly rich in species.
Austria has common borders with the Czech Republic, Germany,
Hungary, Italy, Liechtenstein, Slovakia, Slovenia and Switzerland.
The democratic Republic of Austria is a federal state
consisting of nine independent Bundesländer or provinces
(Carinthia, Burgenland, Lower Austria, Salzburg, Styria, Tyrol,
Upper Austria, Vienna and Vorarlberg).
It has a population of 8,029,717 (1994); average life expectancy
is 73 years for men and 79.5 years for women.
About 98% of the population are German-speaking,
the rest is made up of Slovenian, Croat, Hungarian and Czech ethnic groups;
78% are Roman-Catholic, while 5% are Protestants and 2% belong to Islam;
12% are non-denominational and 3% are members of the
other 13 recognised denominations.
For administrative purposes, the national territory is divided
into 99 political districts, of which 84 are rural districts and
15 are urban districts (towns with their own byelaws).
Of the 2,353 municipalities, 176 have town status
and 697 are market towns;
added to this are 7,835 catastral communities
(administrative units combined in a land register) and 17,234 villages.

The lines printed in bold above the following notes
indicate the title and page numbers of the
relevant part of the picture section.
The text summarises brief data on key subjects
to provide an informative overview of each province.

Güssing, view across a fish pond towards the town and former fortress.

Klagenfurt, estates' house; courtyard and flights of stairs, arcaded gallery and towers.

Dürnstein, view across the Danube towards the former abbey church and the castle ruin.

Burgenland.
Pages 11 to 18.

Location and history have made Burgenland a borderland. It is Austria's easternmost Bundesland (province), third smallest by area and smallest by population; the last to be established (in 1921). It perches between the eastern foothills of the Central Alps (Leithagebirge, Ödenburger Gebirge and Günser Gebirge), the rims of the Hungarian plain (Seewinkel, Wulka plain) and the undulating hills of the south. The lake scene around Neusiedler See and Seewinkel harbours a singular steppe land unique in Europe. Burgenland consists of a low-lying part to the north of the Ödenburg range (around Eisenstadt), a basin edged in by hills between the Ödenburg and Güns ranges (around Oberpullendorf), and hilly country to the south (around Güssing). Tectonic fault lines underneath (Great Hungarian Plain) are a source of numerous mineral and medicinal springs. An agricultural land of Pannonian climate, the province grows wheat, maize, wine (34.3% of the total wine-growing area of Austria) and vegetables. Structural problems (most land was owned by a few big landowners) and a small industrial base led to perennial scarcity of work, successive waves of emigration and large numbers of commuters to other provinces. Of the population, 88.3% are German-speaking, 7.2% speak Croatian and 2.5% Hungarian. At 13.7%, the province has a very high share of Protestants. Burgenland covers an area of 3,965 sq km and has 273,613 inhabitants (69 per sq km); accounting for 4.72% of the land and 3.4% of the population of Austria. Its capital, Eisenstadt, has 10,349 residents. Area distribution: arable land, 39.3%; forest, 25.5%; vineyards, 4.9%; grassland, 5.9%; water bodies, 2.9%; unproductive land, 2.2%.

Carinthia.
Pages 19 to 26.

The southernmost part of Austria, Carinthia is the fifth smallest province by area and fourth smallest by population. Its territory, made up of a mountainous west (Upper Carinthia) and a wide basin to the east (Lower Carinthia), is bounded by several chains of high mountains: Hohe Tauern, Koralpe, Karawanken and the Karnic Alps. Four large lakes (Wörther See, Ossiacher See, Millstätter See and Weissensee) and a host of small to tiny lakes provide the foundation for a particularly attractive holiday area with a very favourable climate (Pannonian combined with Mediterranean). Farming and the mining industry have been in a decline for many years; the large share of tourist and construction jobs causes seasonal unemployment. Timber is a major economic factor (Carinthia boasts the second largest share of forest land); the farm crops (grain, maize and fruits) stem mostly from the agricultural areas in Lower Carinthia and the meadows and alps in the mountains (lifestock breeding). Rivers have been harnessed for electricity generation by a string of large hydro-electric power plants. Carinthia ranks third in revenues from the tourist business. The Klagenfurt basin and Lavant valley are densely populated (50% of the population are crowded on 15% of the territory). Of the inhabitants, 97% are German-speaking. 3% (in the southernmost parts) speak Slovenian. Carinthia covers an area of 9,533 sq km and has 559,696 inhabitants (58.7 per sq km); accounting for 11.3% of the land and 6.9% of the population of Austria. Its capital, Klagenfurt, has 89,415 residents. Area distribution: arable land, 7.1%; forest, 46.5%; grassland, 12.9%; alps, 15.9%; water bodies, less than 1%; unproductive land, 6.9%.

Lower Austria.
Pages 27 to 36.

The nucleus of present-day Austria, Lower Austria developed from a border mark known as "ostarrichi" to become the largest province by area and second largest by population. Situated in the northeast of Austria, it is bisected by the Danube into a northern and southern half. The geomorphological structure is reflected in its historical division into geographical quarters: to the north of the Danube the Waldviertel, the forested western quarter, a rugged plateau of primary rock and harsh weather (Bohemian massif) and, adjoining it in the east, the Weinviertel, fertile loess hills dotted with vineyards; to the south of the river the Mostviertel, an orcharded quarter in the west, with a generous share of fertile foothills; neighbouring the heavily industrialised Industrieviertel in the east that extends over a landscape of basins (Vienna basin) made up of sediments. Its mixed climate tends towards the continental and Pannonian in the east, to the Atlantic in the foothills and to the Alpine in its mountainous south. Lower Austria is the foremost agricultural province. It has the second largest forest area in Austria, almost 50% of the arable land, more than half of the vineyards and, in the Weinviertel, the greater part of Austria's oil and gas deposits. The province is home to 18.9% of all Austrians; there are no significant linguistic minorities. Lower Austria covers an area of 19,173.5 sq km and has 1,511,555 inhabitants (78.8 per sq km); accounting for 22.9% of the land and 18.8% of the population of Austria. Its capital (since 1986), St. Pölten, has 50,026 residents. Area distribution: arable land, 36.4%; forest, 34.7%; vineyards, almost 2%; grassland, 11.3%; water bodies, 0.25%; alps, 0.5%; unproductive land, 2%.

Linz, city square, view across the Neptune fountain towards Jesuitenkirche (former cathedral church).

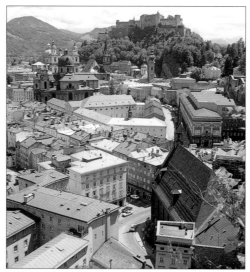

Salzburg, view towards the festival hall, the old town and Hohensalzburg fortress.

Graz, view from the Schloßberg towards Palais Attems, Dreifaltigkeitskirche and Mariahilferkirche.

Upper Austria.
Pages 37 to 46.

The historical development of Upper Austria was closely tied to that of Lower Austria, its eastern neighbour. Located in the northwest of Austria, it is the fourth largest province by area and third largest by population, divided by the Danube into two unequal parts: the smaller northern half, a barren, poor table-land of granite that continues north as the Bohemian massif; and a plentiful south full of hills, terraces and basins in the Alpine foot-hills, backed by the chains of the Northern Limestone Alps. It has preserved its historical division into quarters: the Mühlviertel to the north of the Danube, Inn-, Hausruck- and Traunviertel to its south. The Salzkammergut in the Traunviertel enjoys worldwide fame for its scenic beauty and abundance of lakes. The climate in the province is changeable and characterised by frequent rainfall, influenced by the Atlantic (prevailing westerly winds), slightly harsher on the granite plateau and in the Alps. Originally concentrated on farming, Upper Austria has over the past 60 years changed its focus and become a major indus-trial location (steel processing, automotive industry, machines, pulp and paper mills). It can look back on a long tradition of salt min-ing and today operates oil and gas fields as well. It is the leading producer of electricity. The province has no linguistic minorities. Upper Austria covers an area of 11,979.65 sq km and has 1,383,620 inhabitants (115.5 per sq km); accounting for 14.3% of the land and 17.2% of the population of Austria. Its capi-tal, Linz, has 203,044 residents (the third largest city of Austria). Area distribution: arable land, 24.3%; forest, 36.2%; grassland, 23.3%; alps, 0.4%; water bodies, 0.5%; un-productive land, 5.5%.

Salzburg.
Pages 47 to 56.

Equivalent to the territory once ruled by the prince-archbishops of Salzburg (14th to early 19th cent.), the province accrued to Austria by virtue of the Congress of Vienna (1814/15). Situated in the middle of Austria, it is the fourth smallest province by area and third smallest by population. Its administrative di-visions are: Flachgau with a share of the Al-pine foothills and Salzkammergut; Tennengau in the Limestone Alps; Pinzgau and Pongau in the Central Alps north of the Hohe Tauern and the Salzach valley; and Lungau, a basin on the southern side of the Niedere Tauern. Over 80% are covered by mountains, 20% are rocky ground and glaciers; the lakes are found in the Flachgau. The climate is characterised by a high precipitation rate (the legendary *Schnürlregen*), with the exception of the Lun-gau basin, a spot of extreme continental cli-mate. The rainy weather favours the mea-dows, pastures and alps which provide the underpinnings for extensive lifestock farming. Mining of silver, gold, copper, iron ore and salt, once an important source of revenues, was shut down in the 20th century. The city of Salzburg is famous for its scenic and archi-tectural attractions and its luxuriant cultural offer (festivals); Salzburg ranks second in the tourist business. The city is home to almost 30% of the population. The province has no significant linguistic minorities. Salzburg covers an area of 7,154.24 sq km and has 504,258 inhabitants (70.5 per sq km), accounting for 8.5% of the land and 6.3% of the population of Austria. Its capital, Salzburg, has 143,978 residents. Area distri-bution: arable land, 1%; forest, 34%; grass-land, 17%; alps, 24%; water bodies, 0.6%; unproductive land, 14.5%.

Styria.
Pages 57 to 66.

Located in the southeast and historically an integral part of Austria, Styria is the second largest province by area and fourth largest by population. Mountainous Upper Styria has a share in the Northern Limestone Alps, the Central Alps and the southern foothill chains; hilly Western Styria takes a section of the foothill chains and basins along the Mur river; Eastern Styria spreads from the Mur towards the Hungarian Plain in softly rolling hills. The Alpine climate is prevalent in the moun-tainous areas, while the eastern part is gov-erned by the Pannonian climate. More than half of the province is covered by forests ("Green Mark"), but it also takes a leading role in the mining and ore processing indus-tries. Iron ore from Upper Styria and iron working ("Iron Mark"), coal and magnesite have long been mainstays of its economy. More recently, electric, pulp, paper and auto-motive industries have been added, supple-mented by the industry that has sprung up around the mineral and medicinal springs in Eastern Styria. Farming, fruit and wine-grow-ing are important in Western and Eastern Styria; more than half of the farming income derives from animal husbandry and dairying. Densely settled areas are found only along the river valleys of Upper Styria. A Slovenian minority lives at the southern border. Styria covers an area of 16,388.15 sq km and has 1,203,993 inhabitants (73.46 per sq km), accounting for 19.5% of the land and 15% of the population of Austria. Its capital, Graz, has 237,810 residents (the second-largest city of Austria). Area distribution: arable land, 9.6%; forest, 52%; grassland, 15%; vine-yards, 0.22%; alps, 6%; water bodies, 0.25%; unproductive land, 8%.

Innsbruck, view from Berg Isel across the abbey and parish church of Wilten and the city towards Nordkette.

Bregenz, view from Pfänder across the town, Lake Constance, the mouth of the Rhine and Swiss mountains.

Vienna, view from the Burgtheater across Rathausplatz and Rathauspark towards the city hall.

Tyrol.
Pages 67 to 76.

Situated rather in the west of Austria, Tyrol received its present shape of two territorially separated parts (North and East Tyrol) when South Tyrol was ceded to Italy in 1919. The Alpine province, securely established as one of the world's best known vacation areas, is the third largest by area and fifth largest by population. Central features of North Tyrol are the peaks of the Northern Limestone Alps and Central Alps on either side of the trough-shaped Inn valley. East Tyrol consists of the Hohe Tauern mountains to the north, the Defreggen slate range, the Lienz basin and the Southern Limestone Alps. A moderate climate prevails in the north; the Northern Limestone Alps have a high precipitation rate, while the Inn valley is governed by the Alpine climate (warm southerly winds known as *föhn).* The sheltered basin of the east provides for cold winters and warm summers. Tyrol derives its historical importance as much as its current problems (heavy traffic) from its location at the transit route that links northern Central Europe to the Mediterranean. Tourism apart, industry and commerce as well as electricity generation are Tyrol's chief sources of revenues. Agriculture in the province is characterised by extremes: just 1% of the land is used for tilling, but 70% are forest, grassland and alps. Tyrol is sparsely populated (except for the Inn valley) and has no minority groups. Tyrol covers an area of 12,647.82 sq km and has 654,753 inhabitants (51.76 per sq km); accounting for 15% of the land and 8.1% of the population of Austria. Its capital, Innsbruck, has 118,112 residents. Area distribution: arable land, 1%; forest, 33.5%; grassland, 9%; alps, 26%; water bodies, 0.1%; unproductive land, 24.4%.

Vorarlberg.
Pages 77 to 84.

Separated by the Arlberg mountain from the main part of Austria, Vorarlberg (known affectionately as *Ländle* or "little country") is the westernmost province, second smallest by area and population. Its main features are Lake Constance, the Rhine valley, the peaks of the Rätikon and Silvretta to the south, the Verwall group, Lechtal (Arlberg) and Allgäu Alps to the east and the Bregenz forest nestling between and descending towards the Rhine valley. The Arlberg acts as a climatic divide, keeping the province under the sway of rainy Atlantic weather. The warm Rhine valley is frequently foggy, with *föhn* winds. In winter, the Alpine valleys (Lech, Montafon) are usually favoured by sunshine and have built a reputation as skiing resorts. As in neighbouring Tyrol, tilling is overshadowed by the successful industries of Alpine dairy farming (grassland and alp pastures make up 50% of the land) and cheese-making (from 60% of the milk production). Vorarlberg has a highly developed industry, focusing on (world-famous) textile products, electricity from hydro-electric plants, chocolate, juice and cheese. Two thirds of the population live in the Rhine valley. The country has attracted a large proportion of immigrants. It is the second most densely populated province and has the largest share of immigrants (13.3%) after Vienna. An Allemanic dialect is spoken. Vorarlberg covers an area of 2,601.40 sq km and has 342,461 inhabitants (132 per sq km); accounting for 3% of the land and 4.2% of the population of Austria. Its capital, Bregenz, has 115,500 residents. Area distribution: arable land, 0.8%; forest, 24%; grassland, 17%; alps, 30%; water bodies, 0.2%; unproductive land, 11%.

Vienna.
Pages 85 to 94.

Vienna is the federal capital and a province in its own right (since 1920/22). It is the smallest province by area, but the largest by population and most densely settled of the nine. Vienna is the political, economic, cultural and intellectual capital of the Republic of Austria; the seat of the two federal legislative bodies, the federal president, the federal government and the supreme courts and administrative bodies. Vienna is also an international centre for conferences, shows and trade fairs, the headquarters of a number of international organisations (United Nations agencies, IAEA, UNIDO, OPEC), one of the oldest established cities of Europe and a major centre and hub of art, culture and tourism. As a province and city, Vienna has a provincial diet, municipal council, provincial government and municipal administration. Its history and development were ruled by its geographical location at the junction of major trading routes, European regions and European cultures. Vienna lies at the banks of the Danube. The transitional climate fluctuates between the cool, rainy summers and mild winters of the Atlantic weather and the hot, dry summers and cold winters of its continental pendant. The population of Vienna is a mixture of numerous ethnic and religious groups that has its roots in the large migratory movements of the imperial period. More recent immigrants make up 19.3%. Vienna covers an area of 414.95 sq km and has 1,595,768 inhabitants (3,854 per sq km); accounting for 0.5% of the land and 20% of the population of Austria. In 23 districts, 153,693 buildings offer 853,091 residential units. Area distribution: total built-up area, 30.3%; traffic space, 13.5%; grassland, parks and forests, 49.6%; water bodies, 5%.

Additional Notes.

Dust jacket
The "Fähnrichstor", first of 14 large gateways that are part of the fortifications to defend the access to Hochosterwitz Castle, Carinthia.

Endpapers
Left: Enns valley and Grimming, Styria.
Right: vault of Königswiesen parish church, Upper Austria.

Half-title
The Austrian flag with the Republic's coat-of-arms, flagpole in front of the Parliament building, Vienna.

Full title
Page 2
View from the city hall tower across Rathaus-park, Ringstrasse, Volksgarten and Helden-platz to the Neue Burg, Vienna.
Page 3
Top: Seewinkel, Burgenland; Gradenbach valley near Heiligenblut, Carinthia; Mostvier-tel near Seitenstetten Abbey, Lower Austria; centre: Gosau valley and Gosaukamm, Upper Austria; Osterhorn peaks from Schafberg, Salzburg; bottom: Enns valley and Grimming, Styria; flock of sheep near the Inn valley at Landeck, Tyrol; Lech am Arlberg, Vorarlberg.

Intermediate titles

All statistical data quoted herein are from the Austrian Central Statistical Office, the Stati-stisches Jahrbuch für die Republik Österreich of 1995 and the Österreichischer Amtskalen-der 1995/96. All data are compiled on the basis of material valid for 1995.

Other books by the author:
Published by Edition Hausner

Ernst Hausner
Burgenland
172 pages, 536 colour pictures, 1990.

Ernst Hausner
Styria
212 pages, 880 colour pictures,
also published in German, 1992.

Ernst Hausner
Oberösterreich
206 pages, 753 colour pictures, 1995.

Published by Jugend & Volk Verlag

Ernst Hausner
Wien
308 pages, 865 colour pictures,
with texts in English, German and Italian, 1988.

Ernst Hausner
Vienna,
Strolling Through a Beautiful City
120 pages, 444 colour pictures,
also published in French, German and Italian, 1993.

Ernst Hausner
Vienna,
Strolling Through an Unknown City
120 pages, 363 colour pictures,
also published in German, 1994.

Ernst Hausner
Vienna,
Introduction and Reminiscence
80 pages, 177 colour pictures,
also published in Chinese, French, German, Italian, Japanese and Russian, 1994.

Ernst Hausner
Österreich
252 pages, 842 colour pictures,
with texts in English, German and Italian, 1986.

Ernst Hausner
Niederösterreich
206 pages, 743 colour pictures, 1989.